P9-DCX-351

Medieval Latin Lyrics

MEDIEVAL LATIN LYRICS

*Translated & Introduced
by Brian Stock*

*Original Woodcuts
by Fritz Kredel*

DAVID GODINE·PUBLISHER

BOSTON·MCMLXXI

*Copyright © 1971
by Brian Stock*

*Illustrations
Copyright © 1971
by David Godine*

*Library of Congress
Catalogue Number
79-104913* ✓

*International
Standard Book
Number
0-87923-028-2*

For Béatrice

Contents

Introduction   9

Leuis exsurgit zephirus   18

Clangam filii   20

O admirabile Veneris idolum   24

Foebus abierat   26

Notker Balbulus: Quid tu, virgo   28

Quis est hic   30

Amor communis omnibus   34

Walter of Châtillon: Inperio Venerio   36

Idem: Autumnali frigore   38

Invehar in Venerem   42

Ab ungue primo teneram   48

Redit estas cunctis grata   52

Sol ramium fervens   54

Huc usque, me miseram   58

Rumor letalis   62

Peter Abelard: Planctus Iacob   66

Vitam duxi   72

Introduction

Most of the manuscript collections of Latin lyrics put together during the Middle Ages were personal anthologies. In this respect at least the present one is no different. Its poems have been chosen not as historical illustrations but simply for their own intrinsic merit. At the same time an attempt has been made to avoid the better known, oft-translated drinking songs that have, in the eyes of some, given the medieval lyric an undeserved reputation for frivolity. Medieval Latin lyrics were on the whole serious poetic enterprises, diligently composed by artists of often surprising individuality. The aim of this little anthology is to provide the lover of poetry with a very few examples of their undoubted poetic excellence.

The poems were all written between the ninth and the twelfth centuries; this, by general consent, was the great period of the Latin lyric. Religious 'lyrics' were of course composed at an earlier date; they go back as far as Prudentius and Ambrose of Milan. Nor did Latin verse suddenly become extinct after the twelfth century. As late as the mid-fourteenth, Petrarch, the first modern poet laureate, thought more highly of his Latin epic *Africa* than of his Italian *Canzoniere*. But more than a century before Petrarch's birth in 1304 many lyric poets were experimenting in the vernacular languages.

Throughout the four centuries of its development, the Latin lyric remained a predominantly 'popular' form; that is to say, it often, though not always, appealed to an audience that was oral rather than script oriented. Even today many medieval lyrics display a double character, a simple surface texture when set to music and a more complex poetic structure when carefully read. Although its source material, artistic form and melody were often highly complicated, the medieval lyric never lost contact with the oral culture from which, it is presumed, it sprang. Perhaps this fact more than any other accounts for its renewed popularity in the contemporary world with its increasingly oral bias.

The first poem in the collection, *Leuis exsurgit zephirus*, is drawn from the oldest surviving manuscript collection, the *Cambridge Songs*.[1] It is a well-known poem on a well-known theme[2]: spring is everywhere except in the heart of the poet (or poetess). The handling of the subject is at once delicate and highly passionate. It is, in its way, a virtually perfect poem.

The second work, *Clangam filii*,[3] also dates, it is thought, from the ninth century. It is an allegory written in the sequence form. At a simple level it may be interpreted as the life of man: his birth is traditionally the beginning of a 'journey' over deep, unsure waters; mist is life's obscurities, which Paul and the neoplatonists alike predicted would be clarified in the end; the rediscovery of land is the attainment of paradise. The poem however is not simply a religious allegory. While the fish, which the swan sees beneath him in his flight, may symbolize Christ holding out hope to the afflicted, certain astrological images point in a different direction. When in distress, the swan calls not upon God but upon the stars; and it is dawn, not the creator, that really relieves his suffering. Thus the natural-scientific order is a mediator between God and man. The phrase *amoena arida* (9a) also brings the secular and spiritual together. *Arida* refers simply to the dry land, any secure place, but *amoena*, its qualifier, is associated throughout the Middle Ages with the concept of paradise.[4]

Clangam filii may be compared to two other sequences in the collection, Notker's *Quid tu, virgo*[5] and Peter Abelard's *Planctus Iacob*.[6] The latter two are ostensibly more normal products of the sequence form, which originated as an embellishment to the liturgy in the eighth or ninth centuries. Notker, a monk of

St. Gall who died in 912, tells us in the introduction to his *Liber Hymnorum* that

> a certain priest came our way from Jumièges in Normandy, which had recently been devastated [by Scandinavian invaders], carrying with him his antiphonary, in which certain verses had been adapted to the *sequentia*, [the prolongation of the last syllable of the *jubilus* following the Alleluia of the mass].[7]

Notker's description suggests that he received the sequence in an already developed state. In the *Liber Hymnorum* he brought it to perfection. Wolfram von den Steinen, editor of the collection, described *Quid tu, virgo* as 'sein schönstes Gedicht'. At a simple level the poem's subject is an anonymous martyr's mother; he need not be mourned, she is told, since he is better off in heaven than on earth. In presenting the theme, however, Notker increases the poem's depth by employing Biblical typology, the device by which, in medieval theology, Old Testament figures were intended to prefigure those of the New. Thus, to dramatize the mourning of the martyr's mother, Notker introduces Rachel mourning for her children from Jeremiah 31:15. Yet this is not her only meaning. Leah, who asks her why she is weeping, symbolizes the synagogue; Rachel herself, the church; and Jacob, in the later stanzas, Christ. The essence of the poem's symbolism is found in the prediction of Matthew 2:18-20 which repeats the prophecy of Jeremiah in a new context:

> *'A voice was heard in Ramah,*
> *wailing and loud lamentation,*
> *Rachel weeping for her children . . .'*
> *But when Herod died, behold, an angel of the Lord*
> *appeared in a dream to Joseph in Egypt, saying,*
> *'Rise, take the child and his mother, and go into*
> *the land of Israel . . .'*

Thus Rachel, representing the martyr's mother, thinks not only of her own lost sons, but of Christ,

> *the one*
>
> *who raised up the many.*

The martyr's death is a symbolic act that vindicates the truth of the Old and New Testaments.

Abelard's *Planctus* consist of six sequences. They were presumably composed in answer to a request that Héloïse made in her second letter to provide her with a liturgical cycle at the Paraclete, the monastery to which she had retired after their separation. Abelard chose six Old Testament tragedies to be sung by the nuns of the Paraclete, thus not only reinforcing the spiritual goals to which he had rededicated his life but recalling the misfortunes of his love affair. The *Planctus* do not make easy reading; they are compressed, even contorted, in style. Yet they possess, in contrast to Abelard's numerous hymns, a rare dignity and passion. One of the remarkable features of the *Planctus Iacob* is the accurate manner in which Abelard has portrayed the Old Testament themes of judgment and revenge.

Another partially religious lyric, the sixth in the collection, is *Quis est hic*.[8] This poem is based upon the imagery of the Song of Songs, which was interpreted throughout the Middle Ages as an allegory of Christ and *Ecclesia*. The virgin in the poem, the maid of the Song of Songs or the Church, hears her love, Christ, calling. She goes forth to meet him but finds he is gone. His appearance is a typical example of visionary typology, a premonition or promise of events to come. The central episode of the last lines is based upon the Song of Songs 3:1-3:

> *Upon my bed at night*
> *I sought him whom my soul loves;*
> *I sought him, but found him not;*
> *I called him, but he gave no answer.*
> *'I will arise now and go about the city,*

> *in the streets and in the squares;*
> *I will seek him whom my soul loves.'*
> *I sought him, but found him not.*
> *The watchmen found me,*
> *as they went about the city.*

Yet the conclusion of the poem is different from its source: instead of the lover's being found, he remains a visionary promise. The maid, mistreated by the *vigiles*, is clothed and told she must rehearse 'a new song' before entering heaven or the palace of a secular lord.

The interweaving of celestial and earthly love is a typical feature of many medieval lyrics. It unites the religious poems, described above, with the secular love-lyrics that comprise the rest of the anthology. Among them, *O admirabile Veneris idolum*,[9] a ninth-century work of probably north Italian origin, stands apart as a poem with homosexual connotations. Its starting point is an image of Venus, perhaps a statue. Reflecting on its beauty, however, the author is led to somewhat different conclusions with respect to a young lad to whom he has taken a fancy. What is a virtue in the statue, its toughness, is a vice in the youth, who prefers another.

An approach to love more familiar to the reader of medieval poetry is presented in *Amor communis omnibus*,[10] a poem that makes its first appearance here. The theme is similar to two poems by the great twelfth-century poet, Walter of Châtillon,[11] and to two more overtly erotic works from the Ripoll manuscript.[12] None of these presents difficulties in interpretation. *Autumnali frigore* (no. 9) is an example of a genre at which Walter excelled, the *pastourelle*, in which a knight (or the poet posing as one) begs a shepherdess for her love. In the Ripoll poems, the reader is apt to forget that the erotic was a normal aspect of the love experience in the Middle Ages. The suppression of the erotic in medieval poetry is a distinctly modern prejudice.

Invehar in Venerem[13] (no. 10) is a different sort of poem again. Here the emphasis is on the intellectual side of love, its complexities and contradictions. Its images might be those of John Donne.

Foebus abierat[14] (no. 4), an eleventh-century poem, belongs to another well-known medieval genre, the vision. Even in its fragmented form it is one of the loveliest, most delicate lyrics to have survived. As in *Leuis exsurgit zephirus*, the speaker is a woman, who sees a vision of her former lover, perhaps a deceased husband. The poem possesses at once a simplicity of design and depth of emotion that are not dissimilar to the *Planctus Iacob*. Another, *Ab ungue primo teneram*,[15] turns to a different side of love, one echoed, with variations, in *Huc usque* and *Rumor letalis*, two of the most remarkable of the *Carmina Burana*.[16] *Huc usque* might almost be termed a 'bourgeois' tragedy, since it is difficult to imagine such a poem being written before the emergence of larger towns in the twelfth century with their new society of tradesmen, craftsmen and free labourers, a world in which marriage had acquired a new social connotation. Lastly, *Vitam duxi*[17] echoes a theme widespread in medieval poetry: repentence of the passionate sins of youth and conversion to a more ascetic way of life in old age.

I have attempted in the translations to preserve the character of the originals and not to interpose between them and the reader new poems of my own. At the same time, by adopting short lines and a limited free-verse technique, I have tried to convey their simultaneous complexity in simplicity. As the orthography of medieval Latin is a subject of some controversy, I have also adhered to the spelling of previous editors when their manuscript sources were not available to me.

I am grateful to Edward A. Synan, Chris McDonough, and William Toye for a number of valuable suggestions.

Paris/Toronto
October, 1970   BRIAN STOCK

Notes to the Introduction

1. *Carmina Cantabrigiensia*, ed. Karl Strecker (Berlin, 1926), p. 95. I have however used the edition of Walter Bulst (Heidelberg, 1950), pp. 65-6.

2. See Peter Dronke, *Medieval Latin and the Rise of European Love-Lyric*, vol. 1 (Oxford, 1965), pp. 274-5.

3. Ed. G. M. Dreves, *Analecta Hymnica*, vol. 7 (Leipzig, 1889), p. 253.

4. See L. Arbusow, *Colores Rhetorici* (Göttingen, 1948), pp. 111-6.

5. Ed. W. von den Steinen, *Notker der Dichter und seine Geistige Welt*, vol. 1 (Berne, 1948), p. 86.

6. Ed. Giuseppe Vecchi, *Pietro Abelardo I "Planctus"* (Modena, 1951), pp. 45-7.

7. *Notker der Dichter . . .*, vol. 1, p. 8.

8. Ed. G. M. Dreves, *Analecta Hymnica*, vol. 48 (Leipzig, 1905), p. 76.

9. Cambridge University Library MS Gg.5.35, fol. 441v and Biblioteca Apostolica Vaticana, MS lat. 3227, fol. 80v.

10. Paris, Bibliothèque Nationale, MS latin 11,130,fol. 86r. A critical text appears in *Mediaeval Studies* vol. 33 (1971), p. 269.

11. Ed. Karl Strecker, *Die Lieder Walters von Chatillon aus der Hs. 351 von St. Omer* (Berlin, 1925), pp. 32; 34-5.

12. Ed. Lluís N. d'Olwer, *L'escola poètica de Ripoll en els segles X-XIII*, Institut d'Estudis Catalans, secció històrico-arqueològica, Annuari 1925-30, vol. 6, pt. 1 (Barcelona, 1923), pp. 53; 44-5.

13. Ed. B. Bischoff, *Zeitschrift für romansiche Philologie*, vol. 50 (1930), pp. 96-7.

14. Ed. Peter Dronke, *Medieval Latin and the Rise of European Love-Lyric*, vol. 2 (Oxford, 1966), pp. 334; 336.

15. Ed. A. Vernet, *Mélanges . . . Félix Grat*, vol. 2 (Paris, 1949), pp. 262-3.

16. Ed. A. Hilka & O. Schumann, vol. 1.2 (Heidelberg, 1941), pp. 209; 200.

17. Ed. Peter Dronke, *op. cit.*, 394-5. I have adhered to the stanza arrangement of the older edition of G. M. Dreves, *Analecta Hymnica*, vol. 21 (Leipzig, 1895), p. 156, but printed Dronke's text, changing *neniis* (l. 9) to *seriis*.

Leuis exsurgit zephirus

Leuis exsurgit zephirus
et sol procedit tepidus,
iam terra sinus aperit,
dulcore suo difluit.

Ver purpuratum exiit,
ornatus suos induit,
aspergit terram floribus,
ligna siluarum frondibus.

Struunt lustra quadrupedes,
et dulces nidos uolucres
inter ligna florentia
sua decantant gaudia.

Quod oculis dum uideo,
et auribus dum audio,
heu pro tantis gaudiis
tantis inflor suspiriis.

Cum mihi sola sedeo,
et hec reuoluens palleo,
si forte capud subleuo,
nec audio nec uideo.

Tu saltim Veris gratia
exaudi, et considera
frondes, flores et gramina;
nam mea languet anima.

Spring

The light west wind rises up,
the sun, on its course, grows warm,
the earth now opens its womb,
pouring forth its sweetness.

Cheerful Spring awakens,
puts on his best clothes,
scatters the earth with flowers,
the boughs of the trees with blossoms.

The beasts follow nature's rite,
and sweet birds in their nests
among the flowering boughs
sing of their joys.

While I see this with my eyes,
while I hear this with my ears,
it is as great a joy for me
as, alas, a cause for sighs

for, seated alone by myself,
I grow pale at such thoughts.
If by chance I raise my head,
I neither see nor hear.

You, if only for Spring's sake,
listen to this music. Consider
the boughs, the blossoms, the meadows,
for my soul languishes.

Clangam filii

1. Clangam, filii,
   ploratione una

2a. Alitis cygni,
    qui transfretavit aequora.

2b. O quam amare
    lamentabatur arida

3a. Se dereliquisse
    florigera
    et petisse alta
    maria,

3b. Ajens: 'Infelix sum
    avicula,
    heu mihi, quid agam
    misera.

4a. Pennis soluta
    inniti
    lucida non potero
    hic in stilla.

4b. Undis quatior,
    procellis
    hinc inde nunc allidor
    exsulata.

5a. Angor inter arta
    gurgitum cacumina.
    Gemens alatizo
    intuens mortifera,
    non conscendens supera.

5b. Cernens copiosa
    piscium legumina,
    non queo in denso
    gurgitum assumere
    alimenta optima.

6a. Ortus, occasus
    plagae poli,
    administrate
    lucida sidera.

6b. Sufflagitate
    Oriona,
    effugitantes
    nubes occiduas.'

The Swan Sequence

1. *I shall sing,*
   my sons,
   the plaint

2a. *of a swan*
    who crossed over
    the deep.

2b. *O how bitterly*
    it lamented
    the land

3a. *blooming,*
    it left to seek
    the high seas,

3b. *saying,*
    'Unhappy bird am I;
    what to do, alas,
    in my misery?

4a. *Although set free*
    I cannot
    keep aloft
    with my wings
    in the bright mist.

4b. *I am beaten*
    by the waves, the tempests;
    I am driven
    to and fro
    like an exile,

5a. *crushed*
    between the narrow crests
    of the waves.
    I cry out, I fly on,
    beholding death below,
    not rising above.

5b. *I see*
    the rich food
    of the fish,
    an excellent dish
    beyond my grasp
    in the sea depths.

6a. *O sunrise, sunset,*
    heavenly places,
    wait upon
    the glowing stars,

6b. *summon at once*
    Orion
    to make the mist
    dissolve.'

7a. Dum haec cogitarem tacita,
venit rutila
adminicula aurora.

7b. Oppitulata afflamine
coepit virium
recuperare fortia.

8a. Ovatizans
jam agebatur
inter alta
et consueta nubium
sidera.

8b. Hilarata
ac jucundata
nimis facta
penetrabatur marium
flumina.

9a. Dulcimode cantitans
volitavit ad amoena
arida:

9b. 'Concurrite omnia
alitum et conclamate
agmina:

10. Regi magno
sit gloria.'

7a. *While it meditated*
silently
the rosy dawn
came to its aid.

7b. *With a helping wind*
blowing
it recovered
its strength.

8a. *Encouraged,*
it was now borne
among the highest familiar
stars in the sky;

8b. *rejoicing,*
ecstatic,
it fathomed at last
the waves of the sea.

9a. *It flew*
to a paradise,
singing sweetly:

9b. *'Gather round*
all who take flight
in flocks

10. *and exclaim:*
glory to
the mighty king.'

O admirabile Veneris idolum

O admirabile Veneris idolum,
cuius materie nihil est frivolum.
Arcos te protegat, qui stellas et polum
fecit, et maria condidit et solum.
Furis ingenio non sentias dolum;
Cloto te diligat, que baiolat colum.

Saluto puerum, non per ipotesim,
sed firmo pectore deprecor Lachesim
sororis Atropos ne curet heresim.
Neptunum comitem habeas et Tetim,
cum vectus fueris per fluvium Tesim.
Quo fugis, amabo, cum te dilexerim.
Miser quid faciam, cum te non viderim?

Dura materies ex matris ossibus
creavit homines, iactis lapidibus,
ex quibus unus est iste puerulus,
qui lacrimabiles non curat gemitus.
Cum tristis fuero, gaudebit emulus.
Ut cerva rugio, cum fugit hinnulus.

Image of Love

O marvellous idol of Venus,
made of no trifling stuff,
may the creator,
who made the starry heavens, the earth, and the sea,
protect you.
Oh let no cunning thief deceive you;
let Clotho, who holds your thread,
be kind to you.

I bid farewell to this boy—not in abstractions,
but, with a heavy heart,
I beg Lachesis
that Atropos pay no heed
to the decision of her sister.
My child, as you descend the Adige,
your playmates will be Neptune and Thetis.
I shall love you as I have loved you wherever you go.
But miserable I shall be when you are gone!

Men were created from hard stuff,
from the bones of their mother-earth,
from the hard stones,
which Deucalion and Pyrrha threw behind them,
and one of them is this little boy.
He pays no attention to my tearful sighs.
My rival will rejoice when I am sad.
What a thought! I cry out like a deer when its fawn runs away.

Foebus abierat

Foebus abierat subtractis cursibus;
equitabat soror effrenis curribus,
radios inferens silvanis fontibus,
agitando feras pro suis rictibus.
Mortales dederant menbra soporibus.

* * *

Aprili tempore quod nuper transiit:
fidelis imago coram me adstitit,
me vocans dulciter pauxillum tetigit.
Oppressa lacrimis vox eius defecit;
suspirans etenim loqui non valuit.

Illius a tactu nimis intremui;
velud exterrita sursum insilui;
extensis brachiis corpus applicui,
exsanguis penitus tota derigui.
Evanuit enim, nichil retinui.

Sopore libera exclamo fortiter:
'quo fugis, amabo? cur tam celeriter?
siste gradum, si vis, inibo pariter,
nam tecum vivere volo perhenniter.'
Mox me penitui dixisse taliter.

Aperte fuerant fenestre solii,
fulgebant pulcriter Diane radii.
Heu me, heu miseram, tam diu dolui.
Fluxerunt per genas ploratus rivuli;
donec in crastinum nunquam abstinui.

Returned from the Grave

Phoebus had fled on the sun's dying rays,
while Diana, his sister, rode forth with free rein,
spreading moonbeams among the woodland fountains,
arousing the beasts of night to the hunt.
Mortals had laid their limbs to sleep.

* * *

Last April I saw a vision
of the one I truly love.
Calling me softly, he touched me a little.
He suppressed his tears; his voice failed.
He sighed but could not speak.

I trembled at his touch;
I sprang up, terrified;
I held out my arms and clung to his body
until I was white and wholly weakened.
Then he vanished. I held emptiness.

Now awake, I called out loudly:
'Where are you fleeing, my love? Why so quickly?
Slow your course, and, if you wish, I shall descend as well,
for I desire only to live eternally with you.'
Thus I spoke impetuously and regretted it.

The windows of the room were open;
Diana's rays shone down beautifully.
But I was miserable.
I had grieved for so long!
Streams of tears flowed down my cheeks.
I cried until the following day.

Quid tu, virgo

1a. Quid tu, virgo,
mater, ploras,
Rachel formosa,

1b. cuius vultus
Jacob delectat?

2a. Ceu sororis aniculae

2b. lippitudo eum iuvet.

3a. Terge, mater,
fluentes oculos.

3b. Quam te decent
genarum rimulae?

4a. 'Heu, heu, heu,
quid me incusatis fletus
incassum fudisse?

4b. Cum sim orbata
nato, paupertatem meam
qui solus curaret,

5a. qui non hostibus cederet
angustos terminos,
quos mihi
Jacob adquisivit,

5b. quique stolidis fratribus,
quos multos, pro dolor,
extuli,
esset profuturus.'

6. Numquid flendus est iste,
qui regnum possedit caeleste?
Quique prece frequenti
miseris fratribus
apud deum auxiliatur?

Lament of a Martyr's Mother

1a. *Fair Rachel,*
prefiguring our mother,
our virgin,

1b. *whose face Jacob loved,*
why do you weep?

2a. *For the bleary eyes*
of your elder sister,

2b. *Leah,*
will not succour him.

3a. *Mother,*
wipe your tearful eyes.

3b. *Would wrinkled brows*
befit you?

4a. *'Ah, ah, ah,*
why do you blame me
if my tears flow
in vain,

4b. *since I am deprived of*
the son
who alone
cared for my lowly state,

5a. *he*
who did not yield to the enemy
the hard gains
which Jacob won for me,

5b. *the one*
who raised up the many,
who stood on behalf
of his foolish brethren
whom I, alas, brought forth—
oh what suffering!'

6. *Should we then weep*
for this martyr
who possesses the kingdom of heaven?
With continual prayer
he looks after his miserable brethren
in the sight of God.

Quis est hic

Quis est hic
qui pulsat ad ostium,
noctis rumpens somnium?
Me vocat, ʻo
    virginum pulcherrima,
soror, coniunx,
    gemma splendidissima,
cito surgens,
    aperi, dulcissima.

Ego sum
summi regis filius,
primus et novissimus,
qui de caelis
    in has veni tenebras
liberare
    captivorum animas,
passus mortem
    et multa iniurias.ʼ

Mox ego
dereliqui lectulum,
cucurri ad pessulum,
ut dilecto
    tota domus pateat,
et mens mea
    plenissime videat
quem videre
    maxime desiderat.

Vision in the Night

Who is it who beats at my door,
rumbling through the sleepless night?
Calling me, 'Most lovely of maidens,
sister, wife, most sumptuous jewel,
my love, rise quickly, open up.

I am the son of the king on high,
his first-born, his latest glory,
come from the heavens to these shades
to liberate the souls held captive there,
to suffer defilement and death.'

I left my bed at once,
I ran to the bolted door,
so that my house might admit him,
so that my soul might see in full
whom it desired most truly to see.

At ille
iam inde transierat,
ostium reliquerat.
Quid ergo mi-
   serrima, quid facerem?
Lacrimando
   sum secuta iuvenem
manus cuius
    plasmaverunt hominem.

Vigiles
urbis invenerunt me,
exspoliaverunt me,
abstulerunt
   et dederunt pallium;
cantaverunt
   mihi novum canticum,
quo in regis
   inducar palatium.

But, deserting my front door,
he had already left.
Dejected, what could I do?
In tears I followed the youth
whose hands had created man.

The city guards found me;
they disfigured my beauty;
took me away and clothed me.
They sang for me a new song
for entering the palace of this king.

Amor communis omnibus

Amor communis omnibus
   dulcis inicio,
aliis repugnantibus,
   hoc in me sentio,
qui multa mala suffero,
   palam et clanculo,
ut quiescam dulce tuo
   amice lectulo.
   Oy, oy, oy.

Amor, amor, amor,
   ammirabilis,
tu es hostis omnibus
   intollerabilis
quem tuo vales igneo
   ferire spiculo
subiacebit utique
   graui periculo.
   Oy, oy, oy.

Si modo cernere
   possem corporeum
altare tibi fieri
   vellem marmoreum,
et multa super ponerem
   rerum libamina.
Non ergo debes spernere
   mea precamina.
   Oy, oy, oy, Amor.

Love Common to All

Love, common to all,
in its beginning, is sweet.
What others might resist
now awakens in me.
Openly and secretly
I suffer
many wrongs
that I may find repose,
dear love, in your bed.
Oy, oy, oy.

Love, love,
wonderful love,
you are the enemy
whom none resists.
Whomever you strike
with your fiery dart
will find himself, for sure,
in grave danger.
Oy, oy, oy.

If I were able to see
your body now,
I should like marble
to be set up for you
as an altar,
and to place on it
many offerings.
Therefore you should not
refuse my prayers.
Oy, oy, oy, Amor!

Inperio Venerio

Inperio eya
Venerio eya
cum gaudio
cogor lascivire,
dum audio
volucres garrire.

In nemore eya
sub arbore eya
pro tempore
tellus hylaratur
que corpore
picto purpuratur.

Per gladium eya
Venerium eya
iudicium
dampnat largitatis,
quod vicium
notat parcitatis.

The Power of Venus

*I listen
to the birds
chatter
and while I rejoice*

*in the power of Venus
I am forced
by her power
to desire.*

*For a short time
in the woods
beneath a tree
all the earth
seems to rejoice
in a body
adorned.*

*Through the sword
of Venus
the judgment
of liberality
condemns
what the vice
of restraint
observes.*

Autumnali frigore

Autumnali frigore
marcescente lilio
foris algens corpore
flammas intus sentio.
Stultus ex industria
logicis obicio,
quod duo contraria
suscipio.

Jovis intemperies
mutat rerum speciem;
nulla meam species
alterat temperiem;
totum cogat spiritum
boreas in glaciem,
tamen hoc propositum
non variem.

Viole, vaccinia
carent rore vitreo,
cadunt, marcent lilia.
Sto semper et floreo.
Dum sola sit stabilis
Niobe, quam teneo,
solus immutabilis
permaneo.

Autumn Love

Like the autumn lily
drooping with cold
I am chilled outside
while I burn within.
Wilfully foolish
I protest to the logicians
that I sustain
two contraries.

Jove intemperate
changes appearances,
but no appearance
can change my temper.
The north wind turns
my spirit into ice,
yet I cannot alter
what is written.

The violets, the berries,
lack their glassy dew;
lilies wither and fall.
Yet I endure, I flourish.
Since Niobe, who is mine,
alone is stable,
I alone endure
unchanging.

Dum contemplor oculos
instar duum syderum
et labelli flosculos
dignos ore superum,
transcendisse videor
gazas regum veterum,
dum semel commisceor
et iterum.

Amoris ex debito
me iugo subiciam.
Licet quis, et merito,
reputet infamiam.
Moris est sic vivere.
Licet ergo serviam,
visus michi sapere
desipiam.

I gaze at her eyes,
twin stars,
and the little blooms of her lips,
worthy of a god's embrace.
I seem to transcend
the wealth of kings of old
and yet I am tossed
to and fro.

May I submit, then,
to the yoke of love.
Let anyone, justly,
think it infamous:
for this is my way of life.
Let me even be her slave,
for I shall go mad
being tantalized
by her looks.

Invehar in Venerem

Invehar in Venerem,
   nisi resipiscat
   et dediscat
veterem
   malignandi spiritum,
     quo principiis
       blanditur
     et blandiciis
       molitur
     tristem letis exitum.

Non est grata satis,
ni se Venus gratis
   exibeat;
   nam si venit, ut veneat,
   cum debeat
   beare, magis debeat.

Prius de ludibrio
   Veneris incertus,
   nunc expertus
sentio,
   quam sit male fidei;
     non exaudior
       blanditus,
     unde blandior
       invitus
   et invitor invehi.

Venus be Damned

Venus be damned, unless
she come to her senses
and unlearn
that old spirit of malice
by which I am flattered
with happy beginnings
and, with flattery,
sent to an unhappy end.

Venus does not please enough
unless she show herself
free of charge;
for if she come to sell
when she ought to please
the more is she
the debtor.

Uncertain before
of Venus's mocking ways,
I am now an expert.
I know how bad she is in faith.
When I am pleasant,
she pays no attention;
then unwillingly I flatter;
finally I am forced to rebuke her.

Ab annis cepi teneris
cum miseris
servire castris Veneris
   nec adhuc statum muto;
sed cum sim pene penitus
emeritus,
adhuc me vexat servitus
   et adigit tributo.

In hoc se gessit forcius
quam alius
Laertis ille filius,
   cuius caput inmune
ab hac transit angaria
sollercia,
qui solus Solis filia
   potitus est impune.

Cur amo, si non amor?
Satius est, ut amor
   in odium vertatur.
     Sed absit, quod amantium
     remedium sit odium,
     quod initum per gaudium
     consorcium divorcium
     per gaudii contrarium
   sorciatur.

From tender years
I took up service
in the miserable camps of Venus.
But to date my status has not changed.
Now, almost at the limit
of my term,
slavery still binds me
and demands tribute.

In this she showed herself
more stubborn
than even Ulysses—Laertius' son—
whose head,
freed from servitude,
was spared,
who alone mastered
Circe—the Sun's daughter—
without fear.

Why love, if I am not loved?
It is more fitting
that love
be turned into hate.
But let hatred,
the cure of lovers,
be absent,
so that a union begun in joy,
might not
fall by lot
to its contrary.

In odium converti
nec ius amoris certi
    nec finis est probandus.
        Amorem enim odio
        si finio, si vitio
        per vitium subvenio,
        desipio, si studio
        sanitatis insanio
non sanandus.

No, to turn to hate
or to struggle
with the law of love
is not an advisable end.
For if I end
love with hate,
I help vice through vice.
I am an ass
if,
by an unreasonable study
of reason,
I am not rendered
rational.

Ab ungue primo teneram

Ab ungue primo teneram
   nutrieram
   ut te, Lice,
   prima vice
etatem circa puberem
   exigerem
   et caperem
primicias pudoris.

Fovisti viros gremio
   pro precio;
   jamjam vivis
   cum lascivis.
Septennis adhuc fueras:
   te reseras
   ad miseras
illecebras amoris.

   Me meo memini
scripsisse legem inguini,
   pro foribus astaret
   ne molestum virgini
   profundius intraret.

The Virgin I Saved for Myself

I raised you as a child
tenderly, Lice,
so that, at the right moment,
I might awaken
and pluck
the first fruits of your womanhood.

You were only seven then,
but already
you warmed strangers in your bed
for a sum.
Now you live with lustful men.
Thus have you unlocked yourself
to the miserable
attractions of love.

I recall I held
my desire
to the rule;
I kept outside lest,
by entering too deeply,
I harm a virgin.

Audax virguncula
majora multo jacula
   suscipere decrevit;
   nomen Lice parvula
femineum explevit.

Pubertatem
per etatem
   dum stultior
   operior,
Lice, sexu ducta femineo,
virgo virum nosti, et doleo.

Te futuram
jam maturam
   dum studeo
   custodio,
corpus adhuc impube tenerum
furtim vendis migrans ad alterum.

But this saucy creature
overruled my decree
to admit
much deeper thrusts.
Although a little girl,
she was satisfied
like a woman.

While stupidly
I waited
through your puberty
you, oh Lice,
led on by a woman's desire,
knew a man while yet a girl,
and my heart sinks.

While I tried
to preserve you
for the future,
you turned secretly
to another
to sell
your already mature
yet deliciously tender
body.

Redit estas cunctis grata

Redit estas cunctis grata,
viret herba iam per prata,
nemus frondibus ornatur,
sic per frondes renovatur.
Bruma vilis, nebulosa,
erat nobis tediosa.
Cum Aprilis redit gratus
floribus circumstipatus,
philomena cantilena
replet nemoris amena,
et puelle per plateas
intricatas dant choreas.
Omnis ergo adolescens
in amore sit fervescens.
Querat cum quo delectetur
et, ut amet, sic ametur.
Et amicum virgo decens
talem querat qui sit recens,
atque velit modo pari
tam amare quam amari.
Iuvenis et virgo pulcra
in obscuro premant fulcra,
et vicissim perconexus
dulces sibi dent amplexus.
Hosculetur hos, maxillam,
iuvenis dum tenet illam;
tangat pectus et papillam
satis aptam et puxillam.
Femur femori iungatur,
fructus Veneris summatur:
tunc omnino cesset clamor:
adimplebitur sic amor.

Midsummer

Summer returns promising pleasure to everyone.
The grass grows green in the meadows,
the woods are adorned with the leafy boughs
by which they are renewed.

The winter, cloudy and unproductive,
was long for us.
When pleasurable April returned,
attended by flowers,
the nightingale filled the woods with sweet songs
and girls went dancing hand in hand through the streets.

At this time
every young girl grows hot with desire.
She looks for someone to seduce; thus,
to make love, she too is loved.
Each handsome girl seeks a new love
desiring only to love and to be loved.

In the darkness
somewhere
a youth and a lovely girl
hide their love-bed.
Closely entwined, they embrace each other gently.
The youth, holding her, kisses her mouth, her face;
he caresses her body,
her suitably small
breasts.
Thigh to thigh, they pluck the fruit of Venus.
Then every noise grows silent.

Thus shall love be consummated!

Sol ramium fervens

Sol ramium fervens medium dum scandit Olimpi,
    fessus pernimium membra thoro posui.

Ostia clauduntur, non clauditur una fenestra,
    que placido vento pervia sola foret.

Curas postpono, quoniam dormire volebam,
    sed Veneris flamma torqueor ipse nimis.

Dumque nimis crucior satis alto vulnere lesus,
    ianua cum digito tacta parum sonuit.

Illico surrexi, cupiens decernere quis sit,
    ostia quam leviter qui digito tetigit.

Cumque manu clausas valvas aperire volebam,
    fregit poste seram protinus ipsa Venus.

Venerat illius conductu pulcra puella,
    hoscula mille modis que mihi cara daret.

Flora sibi nomen, quia florida sunt sua facta,
    gutture mella gerens, mellea verba dedit.

An Unusual Siesta

At noon
the hot sun, climbing Olympus,
blazed down through the leaves.
I placed my weary limbs on my bed.
The doors were all shut,
but not a window,
through which could pass a peaceful breeze.
Heavy with sleep, I put aside my cares—
but the flame of Venus tormented me too much.
And while I suffered so,
wounded by an old wound,
my door made a noise
as if touched lightly by a finger.
I got up right away to see who it was,
who had touched my gates so lightly with her finger.
And while I unlatched the bolt by hand
a very Venus burst in the door,
a lovely maid who had come down by that route
to present me with kisses
in a thousand ways.
Flora was her name and florid were
her deeds.
She bore honey in her throat; she spoke honeyed words.

Cuius crus tenerum tenui, quod non negat ipsa,
    insuper et coxas, sponte sua tetigi;

nec vetuit niveas post me tractare papillas,
    quas tractare mihi dulce nimis fuerat.

Venimus ad lectum, conectimur insimul ambo;
    cetera, que licuit sumere, non piguit.

Hanc igitur cupio felicem vivere semper,
    hoc tamen addendo: vivat ut ipsa mihi.

I held her tender thighs—she could not refuse—
and above, with her consent, I caressed her middle.
Afterwards she did not forbid me
to touch her snowy breasts.
To caress them was a pleasure too sweet to bear.
We went to bed; at once we two were one.
The rest, you may assume, was not displeasing!
I should like this happy creature
always to be so alive,
adding only this:
that she live for me.

Huc usque

Huc usque, me miseram!
Rem bene celaveram
  et amavi callide.

Res mea tandem patuit,
nam venter intumuit,
  partus instat gravide.

Hinc mater me verberat,
hinc pater improperat,
  ambo tractant aspere.

Sola domi sedeo,
egredi non audeo
  nec in palam ludere.

Cum foris egredior,
a cunctis inspicior,
  quasi monstrum fuerim.

Cum vident hunc uterum,
alter pulsat alterum;
  silent, dum transierim.

The Pregnant Girl

Get away from me,
I am miserable!

I had kept my secret well
and made love carefully,
but in the end my problem
was apparent,
for my stomach swelled
and I grew heavy with child.

My mother harangued me,
my father reviled me;
both treated me badly.
Alone I sat at home,
not daring to go out
or play in the courtyard.

When I ventured outside,
everyone scrutinized me
as if I were a monster.
Seeing me swollen,
they nudged each other
and passed in silence.

Semper pulsant cubito,
me designant digito,
  ac si mirum fecerim.

Nutibus me indicant.
Dignam, rogo, iudicant,
  quod semel peccaverim?

Quid percurram singula!
Ego sum in fabula
  et in ore omnium.

Ex eo vim patior,
iam dolore morior,
  semper sum in lacrimis.

Hoc dolorem cumulat,
quod amicus exulat
  propter illud paululum.

Ob patris sevitiam
recessit in Franciam
  a finibus ultimis.

Sum in tristitia
de eius absentia
  in doloris cumulum.

They elbowed each other
and pointed to me
with their fingers,
as if I were some marvel.
They pinpointed me as well
with their nods.

Do they condemn me
justly,
I ask?
For I sinned only once.
Why run over the details!
I am gossiped about
and in everyone's mouth.
I can hardly bear it;
I am dying of pain;
I am always in tears.

To crown my unhappiness,
my lover,
for this little thing,
is in exile.
Fleeing my father's anger
and certain death,
he left for France.

Added to my sorrow
his absence
is the last straw.

Rumor letalis

Rumor letalis
me crebro vulnerat
meisque malis
dolores aggerat.
Me male multat
vox tui criminis,
que iam resultat
in mundi terminis.
Invida Fama
tibi novercatur.
Cautius ama,
ne comperiatur.

Quod agis, age tenebris,
procul a Fame palpebris.
Letatur Amor latebris
cum dulcibus illecebris
et murmure iocoso.

Nulla notavit
te turpis fabula,
dum nos ligavit
amoris copula,
sed frigescente
nostro cupidine
sordes repente
funebri crimine.
Fama letata
novis hymeneis
irrevocata
ruit in plateis.

Honey and Gall

A vicious rumour
wounds me constantly,
aggravating the pain
of my own misdeeds.
Your slanderous voice
judges me unjustly
and now resounds
to the ends of the earth.

On your behalf
jealous Fame
acts like a stepmother.
I say to myself:
love more discreetly
lest it is found out.
What you do, do in shadows
far from Fame's eyes.
Amor rejoices in hidden places
with sweet charms and happy murmurs.

No filthy story shackled us
while the bond of love united us,
but when our desire grew cold
you unexpectedly dirtied
the funeral
with your sin.
Fame, rejoicing at the new wedding
rushed the news through the streets.

Patet lupanar omnium
pudoris, en, palatium,
nam virginale lilium
marcet a tactu vilium
   commercio probroso.

    Nunc plango florem
etatis tenere,
    nitidiorem
Veneris sidere;
    tunc columbinam
mentis dulcedinem,
    nunc serpentinam
amaritudinem.
    Verbo rogantes
removes hostili;
    munera dantes
foves in cubili.

Illos abire precipis,
a quibus nichil accipis;
cecos claudosque recipis,
viros illustres decipis
   cum melle venenoso.

Lo, the whorehouse
then opened its door
to every shame,
for my virginal lily
was tainted in the affair
with a vile touch.

Now I lament the flower,
brighter, by the star of Venus,
of my tender years.
What then was dove-like
tranquillity of mind
is now serpentine bitterness.
Now you send away
normal suitors
with hostility;
your bed warms only
those who bring gifts.
You dismiss
those from whom you receive nothing.
Yet you welcome
the blind, the crippled.
You deceive
important men
with venomous honey.

Planctus Iacob

Infelices filii
   patre nati misero
novi, meo sceleri
   talis datur ultio,

cuius est flagitii
   tantum dampnum passio
quo peccato merui
   hoc feriri gladio.

Ioseph decus generis
   filiorum gloria
devoratus bestiis
   morte ruit pessima;

Symeon in vinculis
   mea luit crimina
post matrem et Beniamin
   nunc amisi gaudia.

The Lament of Jacob

Unfortunate young sons,
born of a miserable father,
such is the revenge
for my sin.
My shame is to endure
so great a loss.
For my sin I deserved
to be smitten by this sword.

Joseph,
jewel of my family,
glory of my sons,
fell, devoured by beasts,
to the worst of deaths.

Simeon in chains
cleanses my sins,
and now,
with his mother gone,
I have lost as well
the joys of Benjamin.

Ioseph fratrum invidia
divina pollens gratia;
que, fili mi, presagia
fuerunt illa somnia?

Quid sol, quid luna, fili mi,
quid stelle, quid manipuli,
que mecum diu contuli,
gerebant in se mistici?

Posterior natu fratribus,
sed amore prior omnibus,
    quem moriens mater Bennonim
    pater gaudens dixit Beniamin,

blanditiis tuis miserum
relevabas patris senium;
    fratris mihi reddens speciem
    et decore matris faciem.

Empowered by divine grace
Joseph was potent
to the jealousy of his brothers.
My son, what forebodings
lay in those dreams?
What meant the sun, the moon,
the stars, my son,
and those sheaves
that bore in themselves hidden meanings?
For a long time
I have turned this over in my mind.

Last in birth of the brothers,
but first of them all in love,
whom your mother dying
your father rejoicing
called Benjamin,
you relieved with your charm
the old age of your father;
you brought back your brother's face
for me,
and, through your beauty,
your mother's form.

Pueriles nenie
    super cantus omnes
orbati miserie
    senis erant dulces:

informes in facie
    teneri sermones,
omnem eloquentie
    favum transcendentes.

Duorum solacia
perditorum maxima
    gerebas in te, fili.

Pari pulcritudine
representans utrosque
    reddebas sic me mihi.

Nunc tecum hos perdidi
et plus iusto tenui
    hanc animam, fili mi.

Etate, tu, parvulus,
in dolore maximus
    sicut matri sic patri.

Deus, cui servio,
tu nos nobis facito
    vel apud te coniugi.

Above all song the cries of the young boy
made sweet the miseries of an old man
who had lost his children.
The unformed words
on the tender baby's face
transcended the honey of fine speech.

In you, my son, I received
the best comfort
for the two who were lost.
Equal in beauty, representing both,
you restored me to myself.

Now, with you gone,
I have lost them.
My son, I held this one soul
more dear than what was right.
In your time, little boy,
as you have provided
for your mother
the greatest pain,
so as well for your father.

O God, whom I serve,
bring us together
or unite us with you.

Vitam duxi

Vitam duxi
    iocundam sub amore,
plus libitum
quam licitum
    attendens,
sed a vita
    resipisco priore,
plus studiis
quam seriis
    contendens.
Ut que causa?
    compellor unica:
ne me Fama
    suo privet favore,
dum sub vita
    vivo filargica.

Impendisse
    libet tempus amori,
ne nesciam
cum cupiam
    fugisse;
malis namque
    medela certiori
occurreris,
cum poteris
    novisse.

The Life I Led

I have led
a pleasant
life of love,
more heedful
of what was fun
than what was done,
but now
I am recovering
from my old ways,
seeking
more serious pursuits.
Why?
For one reason:
that Fame
not deprive me of her favour
while I live a life of ease.

It was nice
to have spent a bit of time
in love,
lest, wishing to flee,
I might not know from what.
For one discovers
a sure remedy
when one knows
the evil.

Ergo, sciens
    quid sit illicitum,
redeunti
    non concedam furori,
sed vitabo
    malum precognitum.

Potest namque,
    ne dampnemus amorem,
vel veniam
vel gratiam
    mereri.
Reddit enim
    amantem minorem
affabilem
et docilem,
    vereri
quicquid turpe
    putat, et amplius,
non nihil est,
    ne forte praeter morem
dum carpitur
    fructus Venereus.

Therefore,
aware of what's not done
I shall not yield
to the madness
when it returns
but shall avoid it
in advance.

For love,
lest we condemn it,
can merit
mercy or grace.

For it brings back
a humbled lover,
gentle and docile,
fearing
what he thinks degrading
especially as,
in picking love's fruit,
he may have overshot
what is decent.

This book has been printed in an edition of 4000 copies at the Press of David Godine. The original woodcuts by Fritz Kredel were printed from the blocks. The type was set in Centaur & Arrighi by Mackenzie and Harris of San Francisco. A deluxe edition was printed on a specially made English rag sheet. Copies numbered 1-1200 are enclosed in a slipcase. Fifty additional deluxe copies are bound by hand in quarter leather and numbered I-L. These have been signed by the editor and the artist. The trade edition of 2750 copies was printed on Mohawk vellum laid. Robert Burlen of Boston was responsible for the binding of the trade and deluxe editions. Deo gratias.